T0144985

To My Grandson,

Keiran Jensen

This Book

Is

Dedicated.

Here's to you and your vibrant spirit.

An insightful tale told by your Nana for children of all ages.

Graphic Illustrations by: Lori J. Chavez-Eddo

Balboa Press books may be ordered through booksellers or by contacting:

Balboa Press
A Division of Hay House
1663 Liberty Drive
Bloomington, IN 47403
www.balboapress.com
1 (877) 407-4847

ISBN: 978-1-9822-2193-5 (sc)
ISBN: 978-1-9822-2194-2 (e)

Library of Congress Control Number: 2019901809

Print information available on the last page.

Balboa Press rev. date: 04/22/2019

BALBOA
PRESS
A DIVISION OF HAY HOUSE

I am a **Source**rer

Table of Contents

You are a **Source**rer.

You can be, do, or have, anything at all.
The possibilities are limitless. You make the call!
You have the freedom to call forth either harmony or strife,
by deciding how you feel about **things** in your life.
Thoughts and **feelings** add up to your point of attraction.
Equal to **things** that are now the sum reaction.

You hold great power to summon **thoughts** that make magic unfold
and conjure up **feelings** that turn **things** into gold.

Thoughts + Feelings = Things

What Are You Thinking?

What's on your mind? It's time you review.
The **thoughts** that you're thinking just may come true.
Thoughts about the past and your current thinking,
become a chain of **thought** you're continually linking.
Your **thoughts** form the words that you repeatedly mention.
Whether you know it or not, you've set out an intention.

As your story gets bigger and your plot starts to thicken,
more wanted, or unwanted **things** come and shall quicken!

I am...She is...He is...It is...I am...She is...It is...I am...She is...I am...It is...I am...She is...He is...It is...

My life.

I am.

My story.

How do You Feel About Things?

Your perception of **things** may need some fine-tuning,
regarding the people and environment with which you're communing.
Do you find solutions or problems in the current situation?
Are you **feeling** good about **things** or just plain aggravation?
There is power in awareness of the **feelings** you invite.
Are you calling forth tranquility or always looking for a fight?

Things that push your buttons can move you in a better direction.
By seeing value in **things**, you'll find there's underlying perfection.

What do You Focus On?

When you think of your past or about the present,
are your memories more painful than they are pleasant?
If you're focused on all of the **things** that seem wrong,
your bad **feelings** will grow and become very strong.
You'll strain, and you'll struggle, like paddling upstream,
instead of easily flowing merrily with life towards your dream.
If you keep insisting on playing the martyr,
you guarantee that your life will get harder.

When your joy disappears life becomes very rough,
and **feeling** good again can be very tough.

How's Life Been Treating You?

Look around you, and you will see evidence,
that from your **thoughts** and *feelings* is what life presents.
Your *feelings* are an indicator of a pattern of **thought**,
and the **things** on the table are what you have brought.
Your *feelings* relate directly to what begins to appear.
Ask yourself; are they coming from love...or from fear?

The **things** showing up are the secret-revealing
your very personal gage on how you are *feeling*.

What do You Believe?

Do your beliefs cause you worry, or create lots of doubt,
or beat the drum of the **things** that aren't working out?
The beliefs that you think that you need to preserve,
may also be important for you to observe.
Beliefs are just **thoughts** that you keep in your head.
They're sometimes passed down or that someone else said.

But, you get to pick your beliefs and choose if they're true.
What do you believe? Are your beliefs serving you?

What do Other People Think?

Don't let what others think, be a reason for distress.

Care more about how you respond, and what others think less.

No one can make you feel bad or lead you astray.

How you feel is your decision, no matter what others say.

Other people's advice is based on their own story and view.

No one else knows what is "good" for you.

People either decide to live on purpose, or they live life unaware.

Everyone has the freedom to choose how they experience **things** here.

What other people think, or do, need not be your concern.

Allow others to create their lives; it's what we all need to learn.

Show Them What You're Made of !

You're pure love energy from your toes to your head,
a "body of light," as Einstein once said.
You're connected to all **things** by the energy unseen.
There are invisible magnetic fields that exist in between.
Thoughts and **feelings** are made up of energy as well,
and send signals through your body and out to each cell.
You can surge or restrict your **source** energy, that's always flowing,
through your cells, the tiny batteries that are keeping you going.

You are an extension of energy, in human form, on a matter of course.
Energy flows to you and through you from a much greater **source**.

There's No Greater Power Than Love!

Love feels good; making **love** the most powerful emotion.
Love energy heals and inspires faith and devotion.
You strengthen your power when you choose to rise above.
By forgiving yourself and others, you're a conduit to **love**.
When you let go of pain, your good **feelings** are back on track,
you re-align with **love** and gain all your power back.

Feelings of **love** are life's most vital re**source**.
"To **love** and be **loved**," makes you a mighty powerful force!

How Much Time Do You Have?

Now is the time where you'll find all your power to be.

Take charge of your **thoughts** and **feelings,** and you'll hold the key!

Time is infinite, but an illusion in actuality.

You only have "**now**" to create your reality.

Your future will never be here; it will always be "**now**."

You're **thoughts** will become **things**, and you decide how.

The **feelings** you transmit are how **things** become real,

time to decide what you want and care how you feel.

Create a story worth telling that you and others embrace,

by invoking powerful love energy in this time and place.

Let's Review.

Now, at first, it may seem a little strange.
Realizing that the way you **feel** and see **things** can change.
By evoking more **thoughts** of having, than not having what you desire,
you will see the **things** around you begin to transpire.
As you change your beliefs and perception of **things**,
you will find that your life will adjust what it brings.

You will know without a doubt that you've understood
when your story becomes focused on all that is "good."

Thoughts + Feelings = Things

My life... good...good...good... good...good...good...good... good...good...good...good... good...good... good...

My story.

Feel Your Power!

Your inherent magic rhythm begins to play,
and you realize your inner guidance has shown you the way.
You feel so excited that you can't help but sing,
and now life responds by treating you like a king.
As you appreciate your life and admit you are blessed,
life will keep granting you only the best.
Your life becomes joyous, helpful, and kind,
and it was as easy as changing your mind.

With far less effort than you may have perceived,
an open circuit with your **source** is what you have achieved.

Now What?

Now, you are plugged in; your power supply is much bigger,
and not living small is what gives your life vigor.
Now, the eternal light of **source** that filled your heart at birth,
becomes a powerful force while you are here on earth.
Now, you're generating **thoughts** and **feelings** that put your mind at ease,
and helping your healing energy eliminate **things** that cause disease.
Now, you have the leverage to attract into your existence,
life's streaming intelligence and ever-flowing assistance.
Now, you feel guided when you make a choice,
your words and actions are influential; you're a powerful voice.

Now, like the sun that knows no darkness, you're a consistent **source** of light.
You are a luminary to others, helping them become bright.

Your Divine Power.

You are a **Source**rer. You're co-creating your world.

Life's joy and magic lie dormant until it's unfurled.

Master your **thoughts** and **feelings** and the way you're behaving,

and become aware of the future that you are paving.

Decide what you want, then commit and believe.

Your commands will be granted. Have faith you'll receive.

Harness your power. Don't leave life to fate.

Think, speak, and act on purpose to deliberately create.

Each second, each minute, and each waking hour,

acknowledge and utilize your **Divine Power**!

Daily Rituals

Wake up each morning and put on your smile.

Be grateful and savor being alive for a while.

Breathe deep to give oxygen to every cell.

Stretch your body and know all is well.

Quiet your mind so you may listen and hear.

Trust your inner guidance when loud and clear.

Schedule things that aren't part of a plan.

Drink as much water as you feel you can.

Be mindful of thoughts and how you feel.

Give thanks and praise for every meal.

Write down good things that happen today.

Pretend life is a game and happily play.

Practice kindness in all that you do.

Speak of others, as if, a reflection of you.

Turn on your music at every chance.

Get physical. Go out there and dance.

Laugh with others when you are together.

Go outside. Enjoy all kinds of weather.

Make things that you do easy and fun.

Look to the sky and acknowledge the sun.

Observe nature's beauty and all of her glory.

Keep learning new things to add to your story.

Use your imagination to gain your highest potential.

Focus on your dreams. This is essential.

Help any stresses you have to cease.

Stay calm and keep the peace.

Strengthen your faith and let go of doubt.

Tell yourself often "Things always work out."

Get excited about tomorrow and set the tone.

Go to bed knowing that you're not alone.

Feel deep satisfaction, appreciation, and love.

Believe that you can have all you've ever dreamed of.

~by Lori Chavez Eddo

Printed in the United States
By Bookmasters